CREATING COMPANY CULTURES

Sean White

ABOUT THE AUTHOR

Sean has over 25 years of extremely successful experience with roles ranging from janitor to Corporate Senior Management. Sean is still a Business Owner/Entrepreneur and is credited for creating a entirely new product line now valued in excess of $40million.

A Graduate from DeVry, Sean started his first company based on a senior year capstone project utilizing new technology to reduce waste in lumber processing and manufacturing. The process is now an industry standard know as Thin Kerf Processing. After selling off the business, Sean began his journey into the Fortune 500 manufacturing where he spent many years being trained on traditional managing techniques from corporations such as DuPont, RCA, Sherwin Williams and Kenworth Truck Manufacturing.

Sean left the Fortune 500 world during lean times and and transitioned to a small company located in Athens, OH (home of Heisman winner Joey Burrow).

Since 1999, Sean has transformed that same small "mom and pop" shop into one of the nations's leaders in the border security industry.

CHAPTER 1

THE START

The concept came to me early in 2000 as I was going through the typical management issues with employees. You know the hurdles that we all face with different personalities, including the culture of the company and how that affected the employees, management and productivity. The company I managed was going through some changes plus I had begun to think of different ways to expand our markets and new product lines were in the forefront of my thinking. Our current product line was nearing maturity and although there wasn't much room for new product lines it certainly was highly profitable as well as somewhat stable. With this stability, I was sure we could leverage it into a completely new product line and so I went on the quest to come up with a new product line.

As to not to get too deep into the product line development phase. Let's just say I came with a product line, (BuckEye Cam and BEC Tactical), and it is currently valued at more than $39 million with annual sales exceeding $8.5 million at the time of writing this.

So we have established a new product line and although it ended up being extremely successful, in the beginning it was a real struggle (as are most new products).

The first couple of years with the new product line I could start to see a divide in the company. There were certainly employees who believed in the product line and those who did not. This fascinated me because it was the first time I could see the correlation between how an employee felt about the product and productivity. I cam from the old school of management. You know, lots of rules and guidelines to follow, always looking for process and production improvements, lean manufacturing, Six Sigma, Kaizen and so forth. But never considered how employees actually felt about the product as part of the production or productivity models.

It could be due to the fact that the new product line was my "invention" and I was personally vested in and became my "life's work" to have it succeed. Regardless, I started to pay close attention to how employees felt about the product line and even the company for that matter. It was at that point I decided what made the most sense was to build a team of believers. So from there I very quickly plotted a course to only keep employees that believed in the product or at the very least were not opposed to the product line.

At the same time it was very clear to me that one of the biggest problems I had was all the drama circulating in the company. Some was due to the employees being divided on the product but some of it was just due to how the company was setup to monitor them 24/7. If they were late, left early, took too long for lunch or spent too much time on personal issues they knew they would be hearing from me. That was all everyone had ever known. From my perspective, I was having to spend a tremendous amount of time "monitoring". This monitoring took time away from all the other aspects of the company. As most small companies, I didn't really have time to divide between monitoring and all the other day to day tasks at hand so I began to think of ways to reduce my time spent on monitoring.

So I starting writing down notes and dividing the notes in

categories. I had production, employee and personal categories (loosely but for the most part that is what there they landed). So the production notes related to how we can improve capacity, quality, etc. Just your normal production management routine nothing way out in left field. But when I started categorizing the employee and personal notes I realized very quickly that most, if not all of the issues were rooted in what I now call the drama basket. You know, the mix of personalities, policies and business practices. It seemed to me that in some form or fashion a lot of the drama at the time was linked to the divide between the product lines. As I mentioned in the beginning, we had a well established, mature product line but I was trying to break into a completely different market with a completely new product line. I definitely had employees that were NOT pulling for the win on this new line. So I came to a crossroads in the company and my management style. I struggled with whether or not an employee should care about the product. I came from the fortune 500 and 100 corporate world where most, if not all employees cared less about the products they made so why should I expect any different in our small company. Maybe I was just being too sensitive to the product line because it was my invention? Should I expect the employees to believe in the product and what if I was wrong and the product was a failure? One of our fail safe phrases here in our Engineering group is everything should hold up to an argument (if you deal with engineers at all you will know exactly what I mean). Even with all the unanswered questions I still had to make a decision because it simply wasn't working the way I had it set up. I f for nothing else I was spending too much time motioning employees and that needed to stop.

I guess it came to the point, as it often does as a manager, that I just needed to make a decision on what direction I wanted to take the company. I reviewed my notes/categories and one of the other recurring issues was drama. Drama between employees, between managers and even between managers and employees. So I started working on how to reduce the drama in the workplace. Yes, I know, drama is a pretty broad scope but I wanted to start somewhere and that is where everything seemed to revolve so drama free was where I was headed.

I started by evaluating every employee, manager, engineer and the company. How much drama did each category add? How much drama was the company placing on itself and how could I reduce it? After the evaluation I ended up with several key areas I knew I could change. Unfortunately, a large portion of the drama seemed to stem directly from some of my most senior and talented employees. The rest came from nickel and dime stuff, you know such as policies that really didn't make sense (but all companies have them). So where do I start? How to proceed to implement a drama free workplace and would it even make a difference?

CHAPTER 2

TOXIC EMPLOYEE

Determined to continue with the drama free workplace concept, I went to work on the plan. First item was to address the elephant in the room, the senior employee(s) and manager(s) causing the most drama. Maybe you have them in your workplace, maybe you don't. If you have that one employee that is always the jerk, but gets away with it because they also are the "smartest one in the room", you just found one!

With this discovery, I can tell you they are toxic to the entire company environment. No amount of knowledge or experience is worth holding on to these toxic employees. It is one of those concepts that doesn't really sink in until you go through it. I have spent over 25 years in manufacturing management and everywhere I went there were those toxic employees. The toxic employee was/is almost always tolerated in the corporate world because most believe they "cannot be replaced". If you take anything from this book, understand that toxic employees are the biggest anchor to your company. They are a complete drain on your entire staff and don't kid yourself to believing they aren't "that" bad. Actually, they are probably worse than you think. With that said, if you are not prepared to deal with these type of toxic employees there is really no need to continue reading. By far the biggest success comes from ridding your company of the toxic employee(s). Conversely, it is also the most difficult process to go through. But if you want to truly get the results, you must proceed with this process. And when you get right down to it, all other items on your list of "how to create successful company culture" you wouldn't question if it truly makes your company better so why would you question this one?

Dealing with toxic employees typically means you need to remove them from the workplace completely. On some rare (extremely rare) you may be able to salvage the toxic employee but in most cases I have found that they have become toxic due to seniority and/or skill level thus feeling as though they are indispensable. I am here to tell you that they are absolutely dispensable, and not worth the argument to try and bring them to the other side. I have had to remove many of these types of employees (including managers) over the years and I will say that the first time I let go the most experienced, intelligent, senior manager staff because they were toxic, I seriously questioned my sanity. Its a frightening position to place the company in butt your company will be better off for it in the very near future. Literally, the day after I removed the most toxic employee, the company attitude had shifted. Several dynamics immediately changed. The first and probably the most important was the entire company knew I was in it to win it. They also knew I was willing to step way out of the box and in a strange way they realized some things very quickly. First, I wasn't afraid to fire you if you were toxic. Second, I appreciated your potential more than your experience. The biggest being I was very serious about creating a drama free environment.

What most fail to realize is that employees that are the most senior and most experienced only add value to the company if they are not toxic. If they keep from sharing their knowledge and only use it leverage their company worth, it is actually hurting the company. The moment the toxic employee is removed the other employees can actually breathe. I'm not even kidding when I say the atmosphere completely changed over night. It was a new day for the company and you could actually feel it. The void created in your company by removing the toxic employee is in realty, creating opportunities for one of your other employees. By removing the toxicity from the company the employees weren't afraid to get on board with new ideas. It prompted them to become vested in the product lines because it became clear to everyone I was serious. They were either on board with the concept and started feeling the change or they just left because it wasn't the type of employment they desired. Which that is part of the process as well. I made it very clear, no drama, you are either here to pull for the company or I suggest you move on because there was no longer any gray space left. It took about 16 months for the dust to settle and end up with a staff that were all on the same page.

What's a toxic employee? I'm sure most of you know one or three but for clarity a toxic employee is any employee that detracts from the company's performance. In most of my cases the employee was hostile to most conversations and especially towards sharing knowledge, mostly unapproachable. Sometimes they were hostile towards change or even improvements (fearing change). For example, I had employees that spent the majority of their time snowballing why new product lines were going to fail. They were team building but not in the way you hoped they would. They could have easily spent their time being productive or at least neutral but instead they chose to be negative. A toxic employee doesn't necessarily have to be hostile either. I have had employees that had no real interest in the company or their job. They are nice enough and not hostile or necessarily "bad", just not motivated or interested in being productive. Again this is not productive for the company and causes drama so they had to go. I don't want this to be misrepresented as the environment I was cultivating was one where everyone couldn't speak freely and certainly by no means does everyone have agree with decisions made. More importantly they needed to know they could argue their point and their position without fear of retribution as long as they were willing to be all in regardless of the final decision. I was also managing engineers at the time and they need to, rather

HAVE to argue. It is their predisposition to want to argue and we all agree that everything should be able to withstand an argument in the engineering world. But at the end of the day a decision has to be made and we needed to move past it. I liken it to a family. Because we were close we could argue but we also knew a decision had to be made and we were seeking the best answer (which may or may not have been "your" answer). My point is you need to be mindful that you do not attribute productive conversation (or even disputes) with toxic behavior. It only becomes toxic if it is a repeating scenario. If you are constantly having the same issues with the same person/people then you probably have a toxic situation. This also covers the subject of understanding that everyone you hire is not going to work out. Simple enough concept but yet time and time again I see managers hiring people that clearly should not be kept but keeping them on. I can't explain why they are kept, but managers need to learn to become more experienced at firing then they are. So if you are going to be proactive about drama free workplace you need to understand that not everyone you hire is going to work out and do not be afraid to let them go.

CHAPTER 3

COMPANY POLICIES

C ompany polices were next in line for review. I started going over our policies and like most companies ours were not much different. With that I started wondering if some of our policies could be changed to increase employee satisfaction. I started to see the direct correlation between employee satisfaction and their performance. It sounds a bit obvious to say that because of course the satisfaction affects their performance. But then again a lot of our policies were normal in the workplace but after a review I couldn't really identify any productivity reasoning behind them so the only reason we had them was because other companies did. Keep in mind that we were a small company (14 employees total) but I still feel strongly that these techniques work in larger environments as well. Actually I know they do because some of them are now being used in larger corporations. At the time (early 2000) these concepts were pretty radical to say the least. So as I went through the policies I started to categorize them. Very quickly I realized that a lot of our company policies were completely unnecessary and in some cases were actually holding us back.

Some of the radical ideas I came up with was flex time. Since a large number of our employee's work fell under the batch process category I was able to let them work on their own schedule. Basically, they could come in when the wanted and leave when they wanted as long as they met their production schedule. They worked their allotted time on their schedule not the company's. Have to come in a little late or leave early because you had to drop the kids off or had a dentist appointment or flat tire or overslept? Not a problem. I started to develop the entire work schedule around people's real lives. Of course there is a limit but for the most part the more flexible we became as a company the more productivity I started seeing. Employees that had issues showing up "on time" were now showing up on their "on time" every time and their performance levels were off the charts. I started seeing teams working together and handling their production schedules and they were doing it as a team. They worked around their lives instead of through it and that made all the difference. They enjoyed the freedom and with that freedom they became sold on the concept. They were empowered with more control over their own schedule and what I found was they were much more likely to show up when they didn't really have to or want to because the pressure was significantly reduced. I also found the same employees who would never champion the company or the products be the first ones to defend or boast about our company. What I was creating were responsible employees that wanted to perform at a higher level. It is a very strange phenomenon to say the least, but everyone realized the method to the madness was drama free workplace combined with a flexible schedule was really working. And it was working really, really well. I get the question all the time, "Don't I have problems with employees taking advantage of the flex time?". My answer is no, and it is simply because I get rid of employees that are not able to handle this type of schedule. It goes back to understanding that everyone you hire is not going to work out so get use to some turn over. The employee teams completely understand that this luxury is found at very few companies in the world so they are extremely responsive to maintaining the flex time schedule. It is as close to a self serve schedule you will ever find. The pros severely outweigh the cons once you have the proper employees hired.

CHAPTER 4

PAY AND BENEFITS

This is always a touchy subject but I feel it is important to cover in some aspect. Most successful companies believe they have the best employees. They are not wrong either. Super successful companies do tend to have the best employees. The bigger questions is are you structuring your employee pay on what you can afford or what you want to pay? As those can be drastically different numbers altogether depending on your business models and strategy. Over the decades I have seen several variations on this but the main strategy should remain the same if the goal of the company if longevity. The strategy is to be aggressive on your pay. The employees are your team and without your team the company will vanish. I always refer to the company pulse by doing a "parking lot" check. Does your company parking well represent the type of company you are trying to project or is it sub standard? As the CEO are you proud of that wealth you have created shown in your employee parking lot? Are your employees going broke because you aren't willing to provide them with premium insurance packages? The compensation package is the single most important aspect of your company. You can do all the right things to train, empower and retain employees, but if they go broke paying for insurance you are going to wish you had spent the money. Invest in your employees it will pay off. Hold your managers accountable and place priority on making sure to fire the drama/toxic employees. That is where the savings are to be gained. By retaining top employees and getting rid of employees that don't fit you company. If you view it as creating a culture, versus a company you will see dramatic increases across the board. Employees, even the least senior ones, will start performing at a management level and intensity because they want to be there and do their best. I have witness this time and time again. I have seen employees take their own initiative to get the job done.

CHAPTER 5

Company Soul

Now this is where I separate myself from every other company out there. Collectively your company needs to have a heart and soul. I'm sure your company donates to the local charity or fundraiser. Your company may even host fundraisers or charity type events. But what is your company's policy towards your employees when they need help? Seriously, do you have a policy for that? How would you even create that sort of policy? Can you imagine what that would look like and the man-hours it would take to manage something like that? It would be a nightmare. But do you even need a policy like that? Some would argue that in order to treat everyone fairly you need to have a clear cut decisive policy for all things employee. I'm going to argue against that. There have been times when life strikes one of our employees in an extreme and unfortunate way that you could not possibly have a policy set in place prior. So does that mean the company should not respond? Having been in business for over 30 years you can imagine our employees have had some extreme and unfortunate circumstances to overcome. My approach is to handle each event on a personal yet manageable level. But make sure to go the extra mile.

If you want employees to see the real company behind the curtain now is the time. We have given months of extra pay to the widow of one of our employees who died from a tragic unexpected death. We have paid employees to stay home when they had a life changing event that kept them from coming to work for 10 days. They were certain the company would leave them behind, but we didn't. Essentially be prepared to go the extra mile when your employee have no reason to expect the company would. Those kinds of events are what makes the company become part of the community and even the family in some cases. Again this is good time to bring up the fact why you should not keep employees that are not a good fit for your company. If you are willing to commit to your employees to this level you need to make sure you have the best teams available by proactively only keeping the best employees the payroll. You need to be committed to your employees on a very serious level. On the same turn they need to also understand that with your commitment to them they need to be on the same page. They need to know how serious you are about their future with the company.

CHAPTER 6

NO MICRO

D
o not MICRO MANAGE! There I said it. I cover this topic all the time and yet I still see managers suffer from the need to be the "smartest" person in the room. Obviously, it does help to know your job and to be familiar with all the jobs in your company. But if you are setting up your company structure so that you are always the lead for every department and every area then you are doing it all wrong. I frequently refer to how the structure of any competitive team is comprised. Is the coach the best player on the team? If she is then the team is not going to fair well.

When you think about your company, you should be able to relate in terms of your team or teams. You recruit players, assistant coaches, trainers, specialty recruits and so on. So do you only recruit players that are not quite as good as you or are you seeking out the best players for your team? Do you coach them just well enough to do the job but no more? Are you keeping them reined in so they can't perform better than you did when you were in their position? Are you giving them just enough information but not too much so they can surpass your performance and/or knowledge? Hopefully you can see where I am going with this. As a coach (or manager) you should be empowering your employees with knowledge and the opportunity to perform to their maximum, not yours. Too many times I see owners and managers afraid to empower their employees. I think it tends to be human nature to want to withhold information and just give the employee enough to get their job done, but no more. Most managers want to feel relevant knowing they are still the "resident expert" at their employee's job. However if you can see a little farther in the future and remember you are trying to build something no one else is building then you are going to have to give up that "power". Just like a coach trains his team to be the very best they can be, you need to challenge your employees to become better than you at THEIR job. You might be amazed at how I run most of companies I have had involvement. I purposely made sure I had experts in every area of the company. Sure I knew how every aspect functioned, their goals and production models. But the magic was left up to those employees responsible. Every company I run can operate efficiently without my "day to day" assistance and this is by design.

I originally came into this concept from separate experiences. The first experience: I always remembered how I felt when I was working production lines and had managers always trying to get in front of my parade. I never forgot how much I despised them wanting to briefed prior to the "power meeting" so they could speak intelligently about my performance as if it was their own. I felt as though they were leveraging me to further their own career (in some cases they were). I had experienced firt hand managers that never gave employees enough information to perform at the next level. They only gave enough information to perform at their level and this hamstrings a small to medium size company severely.

So going forward in my management career I become very aware of my place as a manager. I was a coach and my job was to maximize my teams potential. The only way I could do that was to give them all the knowledge I had and not hold them back. It also meant that in most cases I was not the resident expert at a large number of positions within the company. Once I started managing in this way I started to see employees taking pride in the jobs. Going the extra mile became their intent every single time. It seems that by me entrusting in them something other managers never did, it gave them real purpose. I started seeing employees having pride in their knowledge which only re-enforced their position within the company. I want my employees to be the best at their jobs, not me. I want them to know that I hired them to do their job and they need to be the resident expert at their job. It gives an entirely new depth to your company. My job is to clearly communicate to them what our company goals are and how their job plays a vital role in that goal, nothing more nothing less.

In managing most small to medium sized companies you will be required to wear many hats just don't forget to make sure your employees wear their hat just a well as you do. Build them up and make sure you give them every tool they need to succeed. Don't go around finding ways to remind them who the "boss" is but rather find ways to remind them how important their job is to the company.

The other side of my goal to empower the employee with knowledge is so you can promote from within. I can't tell you how many times I have promoted employees from lower level positions to upper level positions based on the needs of the company and my belief in giving employees the best chance at success. Once you fully commit to no drama in the workplace you may find yourself having to fill positions that you were planning on. And in doing so you may find that you have more talent in your employee pool than you ever imagined.

I take pride in knowing that over the course of two decades I have approached and promoted employee into positions that conventional wisdom would not previous allow. Sometimes the best suited people for the jobs don't have the right degree or professional certifications required on paper but are precisely the best person for the job. I have found that getting employees to rise up above "their pay" actually gets them in to positions where they perform extremely well. Typically job seekers are trying to sell you on their abilities. Start looking within your own company and challenge employee to work outside their comfort zones. Some of the very best employees I have ever had came from challenging them into positions they may never have dreamed they could do.

CHAPTER 7

FLEX TIME

Flex Time is a concept we started using about 12 years ago. Obviously in certain circumstances and positions it just cannot be applied. But for those positions that do not require a precise clock in and out time sequence I have found it to be really motivating for employees. The concept of Flex Time is simply that the employee can flex their time to suit their needs. The guideline is to set the goal hours worked per week or every two weeks based on your preference. Usually our guidelines we set at 40 hours worked per week. So the employees on Flex Time had M-F 7:00am – 7:00pm to get their 40 hours in every week. Employees that had positions that could work Flex Time were only required to get their 40 hours in each week. Which means if they had to come in later or earlier than normal for any reason they could – without question. Have an appointment and need to leave early? No problem. Kids sick and need to stay home ½ a day? No problem. All of the sudden we had created a culture that made it very easy to live life and work in harmony. Once again this became a self monitoring position. There were people checking to make sure everyone had their time in but rarely if ever did we have an employee not have their time in. As it turns out, employees were capable of managing their own time very effectively and efficiently. Occasionally there were one or two that caused some drama regarding the flex time which we handled appropriately. The irony of it was I had less attendance issues with flex time than I ever did with a highly structured time management schedule. Flex Time was by designed to work with employees and not punish them for things that were in the most part, out of their control. If I can take an employee who had a long commute or just couldn't function at 7:00AM but they were perfectly suited for 9:00AM why not just have them come in at 9? As it turns out, Flex Time gave employees more than just a time advantage. They really became so found of the flex time that some would give up a promotion just to keep their flex time because it meant that much to their lives. I would overhear the explanation of Flex Time by our employees to non-employees and they were in disbelief that such a thing even existed. It gave the employees a sense of empowerment that they were in control of their own time.

CHAPTER 8

MAGICAL CUSTOMER SERVICE

Always wanting to improve on our customer service and production models I would religiously send employees to popular service and production seminars. I remember one particularly because I spent a small fortune on sending everyone at a time when we really couldn't afford it. It was the thing companies did, send employees out to learn and stay current with the trends and models. This seminar was titled "Magical Customer Service" and I only remember it because for a solid ten years I still heard the employees jokingly referring to "remember your magical customers service" techniques, usually in reference to dealing with a difficult customer. They hadn't learned much other than the phrase was easily referenced to "things getting out of hand". Since that time, I rarely send employees to seminars (other than the ones they are giving to customers). How we learned to handle our customer base was fairly straight forward. We treat the customers like we would want to be treated, fairly. We try to go above and beyond in most cases. Our products are warrantied for a particular time frame like most products. The difference is we may still cover something even if it is out of warranty. We build all our products and take pride in what we build. If something doesn't last like we think it should we will just cover it under warranty. It is all part of our marketing scheme that customers never see coming. I mean how many times have you gotten a courtesy repair on a product that was out of warranty? How do you think that would make you feel about the product and the company? Now you can see why we will do it from time to time. On the flip side of that where we are dealing with a difficult customer and things are getting heated or maybe out of hand how do you handle it? I have a loyalty to my employees first and foremost. We all make mistakes and in some cases it may affect the customer. When it does we do our best to resolve the issue and move on. In those rare occasions that the customer is just being unreasonable (for whatever reason) that is when I draw the line. My loyalty is to my employees. I have been doing this long enough to realize that sometimes you need to stand up for your employees and move the customer along to your competitor. I feel very strongly about this and it is important for your employees to know that the customer ISN'T always right and they don't always get their way. The irony to this is some of our best customers came to us when the company stood up against them in favor of the employee. They eventually realized they may have been out of line and what impressed them the most is the way the company stood behind the employee. It is an easy position to hold when you believe in your products and people. You will find the easier you make the service or return for the customer the less likely they are to want to actually return the product. They will sense your position so it is important for you to make sure the customers know you appreciate them, but you also are loyal to your employees and products.

CHAPTER 9

CHANGING COMPANY CULTURE

One of the biggest assets to a company is the culture. Yet in most companies the focus is on EVERYTHING except the culture. Companies like to focus on traditional management techniques which are of value but they they tend to overlook the employee, the personalities that each employee carriers. We can (usually) that the employee is the biggest asset a company has. Most valued and if managed correctly can very easily EXCEED your performance goals. All it takes is for the "Boss" to understand how most traditional hierarchies fail them from the start. You know the flow chart showing the boss at the top and then all the subordinates below right? What that chart fails to show is how much the "boss" is reliant on the employees. The "boss" needs to understand that the employee is the single driver to their success. More importantly the "boss" needs to find ways to properly motivate their employees.

In my experience this is where most leaders fail. They fail because of several factors, however ego is one factor that seems to be most prevalent. For whatever reason leaders seem to always feel the need to keep their ego in the way which almost always ends up causing their own failure. Maybe it is from years of experience (my own failures) or maybe it is true that you get wiser the older you get regardless I have learned to leave the ego out of the equation. I make it a point to rely on the employee. There was a time when I HAD to be the smartest most knowledgeable person in the room. Because I thought that is what made great leaders, the knowledge was what I thought was the key to success. As it turns out I was wrong, very wrong. I didn't need to be the smartest person in the room, what I needed what to make sure I had someone on my team that could answer every question. I quickly learned that by empowering my employees with the knowledge they could leverage it to enhance their own performance and desire. I realized that the company culture was the key to high performing employees.

So how to change the company culture? First you need to understand what drives company cultures. What do employees really want and what really drives them to perform? You might be shocked to find out that most leaders feel money is directly linked to employee performance. Why? I believe that is because most leaders, owners and entrepreneurs feel employees should have the same dreams, desires and goals that they do so they apply that logic to performance drivers. What most fail to realize is they don't, nor should they and leaders shouldn't expect them to. You should not expect the same drive from your employees that you might have because they are not you.

If you want to change the company culture you need to understand what makes your employees tick. What are their desires what makes them want to come to work and more importantly what makes them want to really perform? Spend time with them, individually and ask them how you could make their job better. Understand that most employees are pre-programmed to say money but if you really dig a little deeper you'll find money is the typical answer because they never really thought of any other options because in most companies culture money (raises, bonuses, etc) are the only options. This is exactly why I came up with Flex Management. I discovered that there is so much more to employees than money. Once you get to know your employees and you've weeded out the non-performers you will can very creative ways to add value without adding cost. You might be surprised to find out that an employee will be much more motivated with getting to work ½ a day 1 day a week so they can spend time with their children or volunteer (or whatever) over a raise. And that little gesture of empowerment increases that employees performance tremendously. It is what they really want that matters and your job as a leader is to find out what they really want. Obviously, you can't always meet their needs 100% but you should as a leader put forth a good faith effort to do your very best. The term outside the box is well used and beaten to death, but seriously spend the time with your employees and listen to what makes them tick. Then do what you can to make it happen, being completely honest and open with your expectations as well as company constraints, etc. and think outside the box. My point here is don't expect the same from your employees that you do from yourself. This is specially true if you are the company owner or senior management. Your goal as a leader should be to motivate your employees to perform at a higher level and to achieve that you need to work with what motivates them not you. I have seen employee's performance skyrocket just because they were able to control their own work schedule. Didn't cost the company anything extra but the gains were incredible. Developing a unique company culture is work. It takes effort and you truly need to care about your employees to make it work. Your goal should be to create a culture that is inviting and simple to understand. Lose the counter intuitive bullshit, treat your employees with respect, empower them with knowledge and control. Your job as a leader is to make sure they understand their importance to the success of the company. You can't do it without them and make sure they completely understand this as a fact. Consulting other companies I'm amazed at the obvious lack of culture at most companies. These leaders are completely oblivious to the constraints they are putting on their largest company asset. They have no idea how to unleash their employee's potential and that's exactly how my companies win.

It's the company culture that makes the difference. How

many leaders out there can text or email one of their employees after hours and get a reply? Not many? Why is that? Without fail our management teams can and will get a response 100% of the time. Why? Because of the culture we have created. The employees don't hate the company, they actually like the company and don't dread an email, call or text from the company. They are actually willing to help if they can. Why? It because of the culture we have created. In turn they also know they can expect the same from senior management. When they have something that comes up they know without a doubt they can email, call or text any of our senior management and expect a reply. And the management reply is not vindictive, mean or condescending. It's life, they have one and it's important to them and it should be important to you and your senior management team. It's ok to have a sick child or babysitter issues or whatever the issue is, it's ok. Do what you need to and let us know how we can help. Once you create this culture and everyone accepts it (which is key) then all of the sudden the employees don't "hate" coming to work. The call-offs dropped way down and essentially the company performance skyrocketed. Employees would take responsibility and took pride in their work because they knew they were valued. Plus they valued other employees and were also more understanding to company culture.

In the start of this book I covered why it is important to be good at firing people and the toxic employee chapter. This may sound harsh but it is just a fact if you want to be able to have this type of company culture you need to be good at firing. You need to create a company culture to allow the employees freedoms and that takes special employees. My employees all understand this. I make it very clear what our company culture is and how important it is to maintain it. Not all employees can handle freedoms so you need to be able to find the ones that fit your culture which requires you to be able to let go of the ones who aren't on board with the culture. Once that standard is set the company will experience less gossip, less turmoil and less DRAMA, which only clears the way for improved performance.

CHAPTER 10

KEEPING IT IN THE FAMILY

NEPOTISM - This topic ALWAYS comes up.... How to handle family in the workplace. I am always asked what my thoughts are about family working together. There is a lot to unpack here so lets begin. The typical scenario that causes the most concern (or should cause the most concern) in small to medium size companies is when management hires their family. There needs to be hard fast rules for when management is hiring their own family members.

It needs to be clear to everyone that there is an actual need. For example, do not create a position just to hire family members. Nothing can disrupt the company's moral and ethics value quicker than creating a position just to hire a family member. As a manager you are not fooling anyone when you do this.

Make sure the family member actually has the skill set and desire to actually work for the company and fill a position.

It seems like we have all have that story – President's son was hired there because he is basically unemployable to the outside world. It's just a crazy and dangerous position for the company. Why risk losing the company to keep your "kids" in the business? It also doesn't matter how great the family member actually is the downsides well outweigh the potion gains if the only reason management is hiring family is to give them a job. I have seen star employees become sub-par performers literally over night when the management decided to bring on a family member under these types of conditions.

So when is it alright to hire family? When there is an actual need and the family member checks all the boxes off. Just like any other hire, but to be clear, if management is hiring their own family they need to be held to a "higher" hiring standard. If you want it to be successful, you need to make sure they understand that they are absolutely not given special treatment and not above being fired. It is a very strange dynamic to maintain but it needs to be clear to everyone that family gets no special treatment.

Managers need to understand that it is very difficult to integrate family into an existing business. If the family member wasn't there from the inception of the company, bringing them in late in the game needs to be done with extreme caution. Most of these fall into one of two scenarios. The hiring is "charity" or "legit" and the test is simple. Was the job posted? Were there actual interviews for the position? Was it handled in the normal procedure for hiring? Are they truly the most qualified for the position? In almost every case it turns into a charity hiring and ends poorly for everyone. I have seen companies go under just trying to "keep it in the family".

Know this, nothing will piss off you entire employee base quicker than the charity hiring of a family member. Nothing.

Is it ever a good idea to hire family? Sure. When they are clearly motivated and the most qualified for the position. No different than any other hire really. The only caveat I personally have when hiring my own family is to be clear that I hold them to a higher standard. Simply because I understand the dynamics that are at play. So "family" needs to be a real performer to keep the additional dynamics in check.

CHAPTER 11

Wrap Up...

The biggest take away from this is for you to concentrate on positioning your company in such a way it doesn't require defending. Create a culture where your company's performance and employees do all the talking. There is nothing worse than having to defend your company's position. The negativity breeds negativity and becomes cyclical very quickly. If you can create a positive company culture two things will happen: You will never be called to defend your company's position and productivity will increase tremendously. It is amazing to see how streamline and efficient an company can become when it no longer needs to spend time with all the self-inflicted time wasting events that are created with non-productive company cultures. Embace the fact that your employees are your greatest assets. Give them paths to go as far as they desire and be accepting to those who are completely content staying right where they are.

You might be surprised to see how well properly cultured companies can perform when given the chance.

It is quite a ride, but well worth the journey.

www.ingramcontent.com/pod-product-compliance
Lightning Source LLC
Chambersburg PA
CBHW030553220526
45463CB00007B/3074